# Billiards and Snooker

*in collaboration with*

THE BILLIARDS AND SNOOKER
CONTROL COUNCIL

THE EP GROUP OF COMPANIES

# CONTENTS

# FOREWORD

In these modern times when hustle and bustle seem to be the keywords to our very existence it is not surprising to find that as a form of relaxation the games of billiards and snooker are beginning to enjoy a popularity reminiscent of some 35 years ago when other distractions were not quite so numerous as today.

Billiards to the enthusiast offers a lifetime of study in technique and a variation of moods unsurpassed by any other ball game. Its limits are unending and until one has persevered and achieved some measure of success these pleasures are not experienced or so easily come by.

Snooker on the other hand enjoys far greater popularity and offers a quicker reward for your efforts. The coloured balls with fifteen reds are very inviting and games are of shorter duration than billiards; the players, being only concerned with potting balls, get the idea of the game quickly and, according to their natural ability so their enthusiasm grows. As improvement progresses so new moves become apparent and extremely high standards can be achieved.

With the vast number of people now coming into contact with both games this booklet has been produced to enlighten the uninitiated and put them on the right road to what can be a most enjoyable pastime or, indeed, an extremely competitive sport at whatever level one's ability allows, involving all the social pleasantries that run parallel to the game. This booklet undoubtedly fulfils the purpose for which it was written and will I am sure help all its readers to further their pleasure from two such wonderful games.

*Chairman,*
*Billiards and*
*Snooker Control*
*Council.*

# BILLIARDS

The origin of billiards is rather indefinite, and no country can claim to have founded the game as the evidence adduced on the subject is too conflicting to convince.

Early in the seventeenth century, however, many specific references were made to a rudimentary form of the game; and in England, such allusions are plentiful.

Spenser refers to the game in his Mother Hubbard's Tales, 1591 and as early as 1576, Mary Queen of Scots, when a state prisoner, complained of being deprived of her billiard table. In 1634, one of the quaint engravings illustrating the "Divine Emblems" of Francis Quarles depicts a form of billiards with maces instead of cues. James I ordered a "billiarde bourde" in 1605 or thereabouts. References were also made by such famous authors as Ben Jonson, 1637; Evelyn, 1674, and Dr. Johnson, 1775. In France Louis XIV favoured the game.

The modern form of billiards dates from the early nineteenth century, the first English treatise of a serious character being that of E. White, published in 1807. The first professional champion of any account was Jonathan Kentfield, who published a book on the game in 1839. He relinquished his title in 1849 to John Roberts, Senior, father of the great John Roberts (Junior). After the Roberts' era, great professionals have been: H. Stevenson, C. Dawson, M. Inman, T. Reece, W. Lindrum, J. Davis, T. Newman, W. Smith, C. McConachy, C. Falkiner, etc.

The Amateur Billiards Championship originated in 1888, and it is now the chief event of the billiards season, snooker having ousted billiards to a great extent in the professional sphere, so far as match-play is concerned.

# THE GAME

Billiards is a game of skill played with three balls and cue, on an 8-legged table having six netted pockets.

The balls, two white and one red, must be equal in size and weight, and measure $2\frac{1}{16}/2\frac{3}{32}$ inches in diameter. Today, most balls are made of crystalate, which displaced ivory during the late "twenties." Each player (there are invariably two only) takes one of the white balls. One of these white balls is marked with a black spot at each of its two "poles" or extremities. This is called the "spot" ball, or simply "spot;" the other white ball is called "plain."

The cue, which must not be less than 3 feet long, is usually about 4 feet 10 inches, and consists of a tapering piece of wood, generally ash. The butt-end (held in the hand) is a little over one inch wide, and the cue gradually tapers to a round top, on which a leather tip is glued.

With this end the player strikes the ball, the tip being approximately 3/10 to 2/5 inches in diameter. A piece of special chalk is necessary for roughening the tip surface after each two or three strokes, as otherwise the tip would slide off when contacting the polished ball surface. The length of a cue, its weight, and the size of the tip vary according to the preference of the player. The balance of the cue is mainly achieved by weighting the butt. The other hand of the player forms a "bridge" for the cue on the table surface.

The table stands 2 feet $9\frac{1}{2}$ inches to 2 feet $10\frac{1}{2}$ inches from the floor and its slate bed measures 12 feet long by 6 feet $1\frac{1}{2}$ inches wide. This slate bed is incorporated in an elaborate wooden frame, the bed being covered with a tightly-stretched West of England woollen cloth, which has a thickish nap, running from the bottom to the top end of the table. There are six pockets, one at each corner, and one exactly in the middle of each long side. Resilient rubber cushions, measuring not more than 2 inches or less than $1\frac{1}{2}$ inches in depth (see foot of page 6), and with a maximum width at the top surface – they slope inwards from the outer edge – of 2 inches, enclose the playing area, which, allowing for the 2-inch width referred to, comprises the actual dimensions of the table as given above. There is, of course, a gap in the cushion at each place where a pocket is situated, to allow the ball to enter.

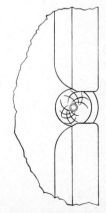

12'

6' 1½"

2' 9½"
TO
2' 10½"

*The Table
and Pockets*

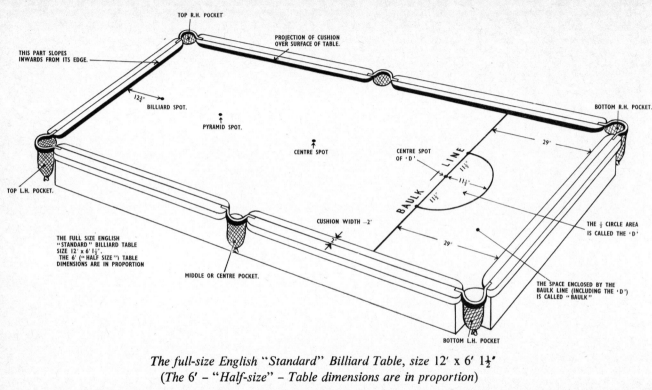

THIS PART SLOPES
INWARDS FROM ITS EDGE.

TOP R.H. POCKET

PROJECTION OF CUSHION
OVER SURFACE OF TABLE.

12½"

BILLIARD SPOT.

PYRAMID SPOT.

CENTRE SPOT

BOTTOM R.H. POCKET.

TOP L.H. POCKET.

CENTRE SPOT
OF 'D'

BAULK LINE

11½"
11½"
11½"

29"

THE ½ CIRCLE AREA
IS CALLED THE 'D'

THE FULL SIZE ENGLISH
"STANDARD" BILLIARD TABLE
SIZE 12' x 6' 1½".
THE 6' ("HALF SIZE") TABLE
DIMENSIONS ARE IN PROPORTION

CUSHION WIDTH —2"

2"

29"

THE SPACE ENCLOSED BY THE
BAULK LINE (INCLUDING THE 'D')
IS CALLED "BAULK"

MIDDLE OR CENTRE POCKET.

BOTTOM L.H. POCKET.

*The full-size English "Standard" Billiard Table, size 12' x 6' 1½"*
*(The 6' – "Half-size" – Table dimensions are in proportion)*

*With cushion overhang of 2", playing surface is 11' 8" x 5' 9½", with 1½" overhang, 11' 9" x 5' 10½".*

## THE MARKING OF THE TABLE

The playing area is marked in the following way:-

A line is drawn across the table width parallel with the bottom cushion, exactly 29 inches from its face. This is called the "baulk line," and the space within is "baulk." From the centre point of this line, a semi-circle (within the baulk area) is marked with a radius of $11\frac{1}{2}$ inches. This is called the "D", and when the player is "in hand," that is when his ball is off the table (before commencing the game, or after his ball has entered a pocket), he must take his next stroke from the "D" area; any point can be chosen, either on the baulk line, or within the semi-circular area. He must not play *into* the baulk area but *away* from it.

The other markings consist of four "spots" on the imaginary central longitudinal line of the table. These spots, marked with very small wafer-like pieces of silk, or by chalk, are positioned as follows:-

At the centre of the "D" semi-circle.

At the centre of the table itself; called the "centre spot."

Halfway between the centre spot and the face of the top end cushion: called the "pyramid spot."

Twelve and three-quarter inches from the face of the cushion: called the "billiard spot."

*Note.* The left-hand spot of the "D" is not used in billiards; the right-hand spot only in one case (see page 15).

## HOW THE GAME IS PLAYED

To decide which player takes "spot," and which "plain," both either toss up or "string" for the privilege, although, apart from personal fancy, there is no real advantage in playing with one ball or the other. Winning the toss or "string," however, gives the winner the choice of playing first, or requesting his opponent to do so.

*Note.* "To string." Each player directs a white ball from the baulk line to the top cushion, with the object of causing it to remain as near the bottom cushion as possible whether it reach the bottom cushion and rebound from it or not. The player whose ball remains nearer to this cushion wins the "string."

## LENGTH OF GAME

With regard to the duration of a game, there are two systems:-

(a) The winner is the player who reaches a fixed number of points (e.g., 100, 250, 500, etc., etc.)

(b) The winner is the player who leads after the expiration of a certain period of time (1 hour, 2 hours, 4 hours – composed of two 2-hour sessions).

## SCORING

The object of the game is to score more points than your opponent. The cue-ball must be struck with the cue-tip and not pushed. A push is a foul. Points are scored by means of three types of stroke, which are :-

1.      The Cannon. A cannon is scored by the player striking his ball with his cue-tip (the player's ball is called the "cue-ball"), and causing it to contact the other two balls, i.e., the opponent's white (called the "object-white") and the red, or vice versa, in turn – 2 points.

2.      The Losing Hazard, "loser" or "in-off." A losing hazard is made by striking the cue-ball and causing it to enter a pocket after contact with one of the other two balls. A "Loser" off the object-white scores 2 points; off the red ball, 3 (respectively called a white loser and a red loser).

3.      The Winning Hazard, or the "pot." A winning hazard is made by striking the cue-ball to contact one of the two object-balls and cause the object-ball to enter a pocket. For "potting" the white, the player scores 2 points; for potting the red, 3.
        *Note*. A player pots the white only for defensive purposes, as when it enters a pocket it stays off the table until the opponent plays, thus limiting the possibilities of further scoring. The red ball, however, is placed on the billiard spot after being potted.

In all diagrams the broken lines indicate the paths of the object balls; the solid line, that of the cue-ball.

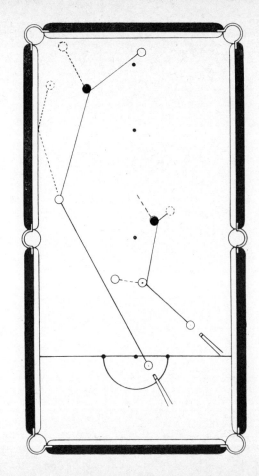

1

1. *Cannon:*
   *The player makes his ball contact white then red.*

2. *Losing Hazard:*
   *The player directs the cue-ball into a middle pocket after contact with the red ball.*

3. *Winning Hazard:*
   *The player directs the red ball into middle pocket, his cue-ball coming to rest near pocket.*

*No. 2 stroke represents the basic stroke of the game, the "half-ball" shot, whereby the player aims through the centre of the cue-ball at the outer rim of the object-ball. From this angle countless other "angles" are estimated. The angle will soon be learned by a little practice. "Side" (striking either right or left of the cue-ball's centre) increases or reduces the half-ball angle. (see pages 22 and 34)*

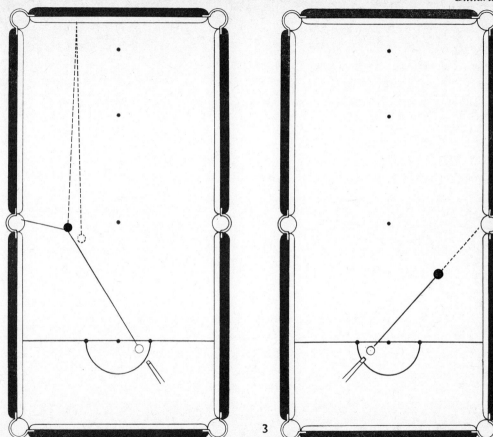

2    3

It is possible to score a cannon and a losing hazard or a winning hazard (pot), or even both, in the same stroke, but such combinations are generally accidental ("flukes"), except in a few instances, when a 5- or 6-shot is profitable. If the player makes a cannon and a losing or winning hazard on one stroke, he scores two points for the cannon and 2 for the hazard, if the white ball was struck first in the cannon, and 3, if the red. The most common "combination" shot is that by which the player pots the red, and follows in (a loser) with the cue-ball in order to get the "D," (6 points).

*Note.* An example of a "fluke" would be a stroke whereby the player, intending to make a loser off the red, missed and made a cannon. Good players have few flukes; bad players, many.

The total number of points scored by a player by a series of such scoring strokes is called a "break," e.g., a break of 50, or a 50-break.

*Note.* The striker is the player in play; the non-striker, the player not in play.

It is not compulsory to try to score, for an unfavourable position of the balls may favour a defensive stroke. When a player, in the course of his turn at the table, fails to make a scoring strike, he is said to have "broken down" and his opponent then takes his turn.

## THE OPENING SHOTS

At the commencement of the game, the red ball is placed on the billiard spot and the opponent's ball is "in hand," i.e., not on the table.

The player starting the game places his ball in the "D" (wherever he choses), must direct it out of the baulk line or area and must hit the red.

If red is sent into baulk and the cue-ball to the side cushion, with the object white out of baulk the second player has a ball to play at.

*Note.* "On" – in a good (scoring) position; "Safe" – in a bad.

*A recognised
opening shot.*

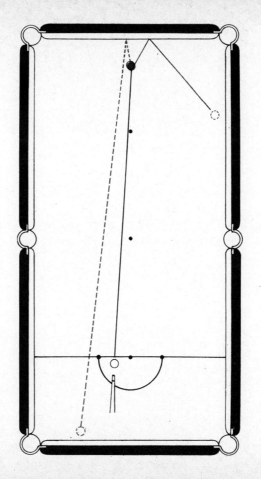

# THE BAULK AREA

A player, whenever "in hand" (i.e., when his ball is off the table), must play out of the "D" from some point within it, that is, he must play away from baulk and not (with one exception) into it. If one or both the object-balls are in the baulk area, they cannot be played at directly. If one is in, and the other out, of the baulk area, the player may play at the latter but not at the former.

It follows, therefore, that if no chance of a score exists, the player can obtain an advantage, and the initiative, by potting the white ball, and placing the red and the cue-ball "in baulk" so that should his opponent fail to disturb them by his stroke out of baulk, he may have a losing hazard left.

The exception referred to above is that a player may play into baulk against a cushion to strike a ball out of baulk.

The red ball is the more important of the two object-balls, for the simple reason that it counts 3 instead of 2, and must always be replaced on the table when pocketed, whereas, as stated before, the object-white stays in the pocket if potted, until the opponent's turn arrives. To "lose the white," therefore, is a big handicap unless one is employing defensive tactics, and not trying to score, as it means the player has only the red left.

The white is often lost unintentionally.

When the red is pocketed (or forced off the table) it must be replaced on the billiard spot. If the spot is occupied by another ball, the red must be replaced on the pyramid spot and, if that spot is occupied, on the centre spot. The limitation of consecutive hazards (15), winning or losing, now allows a player to make 5 consecutive winning hazards off the billiard spot. He must then make a cannon, or a cannon in conjunction with a hazard or hazards, after 5.

*Note.* The rules refer to other contingencies, but the above states the basic principle of spotting the red when potted – or if forced off the table (which is a foul).

When a ball is forced off the table, the next player has the choice of playing from the position left or he may have the balls "spotted".

Every time the cue-ball enters a pocket, the player ("in hand") goes to the bottom end of the table and plays from the "D."

A player fails to score and gives way to his opponent if his stroke does not result in a cannon, a losing hazard or a winning hazard.

A miss (i.e. when the player makes a stroke without contacting another ball) is a foul except when the striker is in hand and there is no ball out of baulk. Every miss incurs a penalty of 1 point, which is added to the opponent's score. Unless the cue ball goes into a pocket when a penalty of 3 points is incurred.

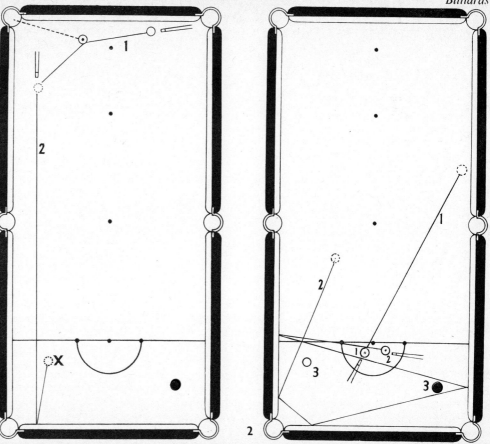

1. *As a miss is now a foul stroke (see "Chief Fouls in Billiards", page 14, "J"), "unless the striker is in hand and there is no ball out of baulk", Diagram 1 shows a miss (after potting white) made to put the cue-ball in position for a red loser. This is against the said rule and is shown to illustrate a miss now not permitted by the Rules.*

2. *Here the striker is in hand and there is no ball out of baulk, so that the stroke is in order. Stroke 1 is the miss which is now in order; stroke 2 tries to disturb the red ball but fails and the opponent is left with the red in nice position for the losing hazard.*

## THE ART OF THE GAME

The art of the game consists of:-

(*a*)    attaining a high standard of stroke play (i.e., ability to perform the various types of stroke);

(*b*)    ball-control: that is, making a scoring stroke with the requisite degree of strength and accuracy to ensure a favourable position for another scoring stroke. Thus, when the player is about to make his stroke, he must have two objectives in view: to make the scoring stroke (i.e., achieve the loser, pot or cannon, as the case may be); and to leave the balls in a suitable position for another scoring stroke. A favourable position for scoring is called a "good leave;" an unfavourable one, a "bad leave."

Indifferent players hit too hard and concern themselves mainly with the first objective, scoring; good players concentrate mainly on the "leave," as they take the score for granted. In short, if the player's technique is such that every stroke appears easy to the onlooker (so as to cause the latter to think, "I could do any of the strokes"), he can be said to be playing high-class billiards.

Artistry, therefore, is accuracy plus nicely-gauged ball control. In other words, a break consists of a chain of interrelated strokes, one leading to another.

## CHIEF FOULS IN BILLIARDS

(*a*)    If the cue-ball is "pushed" with the cue, instead of being struck.

(*b*)    If a ball (or balls) is forced off the table.

(*c*)    If a stroke is played with *both* feet off the floor.

(*d*)    If the stroke is made before the balls have come to rest.

(*e*)    If the ball is touched other than with the cue-tip (i.e., hand, dress, etc.)

(*f*)    If a player plays his ball into baulk when in hand and fails to come out of baulk.

(*g*)    If a player touches his ball with his cue tip before he has delivered his stroke.

(*h*)    If he plays with the wrong ball.

(*i*)    If he plays with the cue-ball touching an object-ball (in such cases the balls are "spotted." "Spotting the balls" means that the object-white is placed on the "centre spot," the red on the "billiard spot," while the player plays from hand, i.e., the "D").

(*j*)    A miss is a foul unless the striker is in hand and there is no ball out of baulk.

When a foul is awarded by the referee, the opponent has the option of playing from the position of the balls left as a result of the foul, or of having the balls spotted, and playing from hand.

# RESTRICTIONS

A player must not make more than 15 winning or losing hazards in succession; after this he must make a cannon or lose his turn. If a player runs a "coup" it is a foul and forfeits 3 points and the non-striker can then have the balls spotted if he wishes. Having the white ball spotted after 15 hazards can only occur if the non-striker does not have the balls spotted after the foul, i.e., running the "coup."

A "line-ball" is one that rests on the baulk-line and cannot, therefore, be played at directly by a player in hand.

A player must not make more than 75 consecutive direct cannons; after this, the break shall only be continued by the intervention of a hazard or a cannon in conjunction with a hazard.

The baulk-line rule has been deleted.

It is not permissible in either game, Billiards or Snooker, to use a dead ball to test whether a ball will pass another, or go on a spot, or for any other purpose. The penalty is 3 away.

A player may seek the referee's decision on a point of fact. He may not ask him for what amounts to advice.

In championship play, 15 hazards is the limit. (15 is now the limit for all games). The referee warns the player at 10 (15 hazards).

# THE REFEREE

As in other games, a referee superintends the play and he is the sole judge of conformity to, or infringements of, the rules. In big games he is assisted by a marker who controls the score board. The referee not only ensures adherance to the rules, but takes the balls out of the pockets for the players, and "spots" or returns them to the player at the baulk-end as necessary. He also hands the rest to the player when needed, and always calls the score.

The referee must declare all fouls directly he perceives them. If he has not seen a stroke fully, he may ask nearby spectators for confirmation of the particular occurrence.

He must be careful not to obstruct the player's line of vision, facility of stroke, etc.

He must award a free ball immediately, not needing to wait for the player to appeal.

# THE RESTS

There are certain "positions" (i.e., of the balls) in which favourable access to the cue-ball is difficult or impossible. For these, a "rest" (of which there are different lengths) is provided, a metal cross at its end enabling the cue-end to slide as normally, i.e., on the bridge made with the player's hand (see diagram). There are short and long rests (called the "half-butt rest" and the "long rest") for each of which a long cue is provided. There are also positions in which the player cannot contact his cue-ball easily because of the closeness of another ball in front of it. To surmount this difficulty, the player uses the "spider" rest, which is a cue-slide of extra height, with a long "handle" like the other rests.

# THE HALF-BALL SHOT

The "half-ball" shot is the basis of "losing hazard" play. The player takes aim at the outside edge of the object-ball through the centre of his ball (the cue ball). This stroke is subject to variations, whereby a fuller or lesser contact is made according to the position of the object-ball, the player having sometimes to "run through" the latter, i.e., cause his ball to take the object-ball very thickly and pass over the space it occupied.

# TYPES OF PLAY

"LOSING HAZARD" or "LOSER PLAY": This is the kind of play favoured by most amateurs. The player aims at making as many losing hazards as he can, with cannons and pots to leave such strokes when a loser is not practicable. It is a combination of hazards (losing and winning) and cannons. It is also called "all-round" play.

"CLOSE-CANNON" PLAY or "NURSERY CANNONS": A form of cannon play whereby the player scores a sequence of cannons with the three balls close to the cushion. Not more than 75 "direct" cannons must be made, as stated before. Very few players are masters of this. Only by close cannon play (also called "nursery cannons" or "nurseries") can such a sequence be made. In the open (i.e., away from the cushions) sequences of more than 3 or 4 cannons are rarely made.

"TOP-OF-THE-TABLE" PLAY: A combination of pots of the red ball and cannon-play, with the billiard spot as the focal point of the strategy. A favourite "top-of-the-table" position:-

The player cannons, sends the red ball towards the opposite pocket for a pot, and then tries to leave another cannon of similar type from the other side of the table. This alternate pot-and-cannon play, however, is extremely difficult and generally, an extra pot from the spot, or a second cannon, comes into the scheme. Top-of-the-table play is much more difficult than the all-round, "open" or "loser" game.

Cue-Rest     Spider     Butt       Cue-rest in use        Spider **in use**

Good "Top-of-the-table" position        Half-Ball Shot

30°

# EXAMPLES OF A BREAK IN BILLIARDS

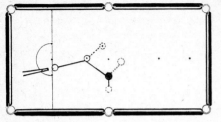

1. Soft cannon to leave another: 2 points.

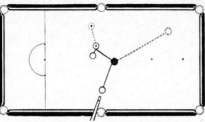

2. Cannon, to send white near middle pocket for a loser, and red towards top pocket: 4 (total).

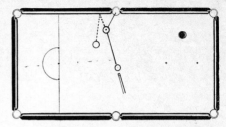

3. White loser into middle pocket, to leave cannon: 6. (This loser is an example of the "run-through" stroke.)

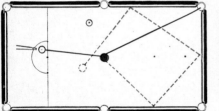

7. Long Loser, fairly forceful, to get red near white; red, however, though well down table, is on opposite side to white. So a further stroke must be made to bring it near white: 17.

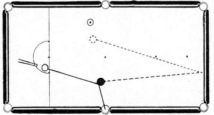

8. Another middle pocket loser, this time hard enough to bring red to white: 20.

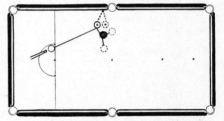

9. A soft cannon but white still left unfavourable, as one does not want to pot it and a loser off it is not "on" i.e., practicable): 22.

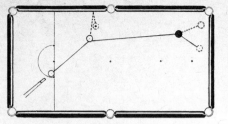

4. Cannon off white, to drive red near pocket: (gentle stroke) 8.

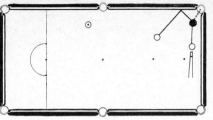

5. Pot-red (which is replaced on billiard spot) to leave loser into opposite top pocket: 11.

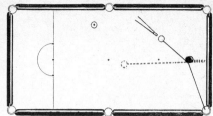

6. Loser off red to bring red down table near white to rescue white from unfavourable position, but inadequate strength used: 14.

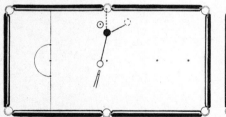

10. Red potted to leave loser off red on its spot: 25. (*Note.* The strokes in this break are selected merely to denote the connection between strokes, and do not represent the policy of an advanced player.)

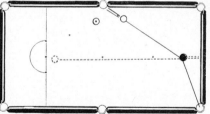

11. Loser off red, on the billiard spot, at last bringing red down table for a cannon which will rescue the white: 28.

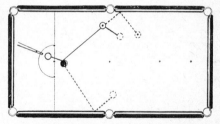

12. The cannon is made bringing white out from the cushion, making a white loser possible, and red also is left favourably. Thirty points scored and position perfect for continuing.

*Billiards*

1. **Left leg thrust forward slightly bent; back leg more** or less at right angles to it; both feet firmly planted; weight equally distributed between the two feet; body inclined easily and comfortably.

2. Head well down, as near to the ideal position as possible, in which the cue almost touches, or actually does touch, the chin.

3. Left arm as straight as possible out on the table.

4. Right forearm perpendicular.

5. Eyes should glance straight along the cue in its course to the object-ball.

6. Cue-action must be as near to absolute horizontal as possible; with piston-like movement.

## THE STANCE FOR BOTH GAMES

The player should stand in the following way, the differing heights of individuals and their physical peculiarities, of course, often necessitating variations of some detail or other. Tall players obviously encounter greater difficulty in attaining the ideal stance than short ones or those of middle stature :

7. The "bridge" or position assumed by the hand on which the cue-ball rests must be firm and the distance from it to the ball should be about 12 to 15 inches.

8. Cue should move freely, without deviation to either side, the fewer to-and-fro motions the better.

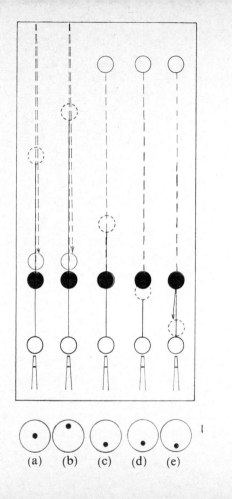

Applying to both Billiards and Snooker:

(*a*) *Plain Striking:* Hitting the cue-ball dead centre.

(*b*) *Top*: Hitting the cue-ball high up promotes extra forward rotation: contact between top and centre.

(*c*) *Bottom:* Hitting the cue-ball low down (i.e., halfway between bottom and centre), retards forward motion.

(*d*) *Stab:* A sharp, stunning stroke, to make the cue-ball stop dead and remain on the spot previously occupied by the object-ball.

*Stun:* Similar to stab, a heavy, deadening stroke when it is desired to leave the cue-ball nearby after contact.

(*e*) *Screw:* The player hits the cue-ball low and with follow-through motion, causing it to take an angle less than the natural angle after contact.

*Screw-back:* The same kind of stroke, but intended to impart a direct recoil or backward motion, towards the striker.

The diagrams in Fig. 1 do not represent specific billiard strokes, but are intended only to convey roughly the effect of each technical feature, taking the plain strike (*a*) as the norm.

Thus, in relation thereto (*b*) shows the extra momentum given to the cue-ball by "top;" (*c*) the decreased momentum when "bottom" is applied; (*d*) the effect of stun and stab which causes the cue-ball to stop nearby; and (*e*) how the cue-ball recoils in a screw-back stroke.

Fig. 2 shows the course of the cue-ball in a right-angle screw cannon, half-ball contact.

*Side:* Hitting the cue-ball on its right or left side to increase or decrease the throw-off of the half-ball stroke. Travelling with the nap, the cue-ball veers appreciably in the direction of the side, the deviation accentuating when contact is made with the object-ball. Side modifies the angle resulting from plain striking and half-ball contact. Against the nap, right-hand side results in a slight veering of the cue-ball to the left. To apply side, keep the cue straight as in plain striking.

Suppose the object-ball to be on the centre spot and the cue-ball on the centre-spot of the "D," and that the player intends to make a half-ball contact on the right-hand side of the object-ball. In this case, right (or "running") side will result in the cue-ball deviating from the object-ball at a *wider* angle than that of the half-ball angle; left (or "check") side, however, will cause the ball to deviate at an angle that is *narrower* than the half-ball angle.

In the diagram (1), "With the Nap," the broken line shows the path of a plain half-ball stroke, the solid line, that of a stroke with running side (i.e., right-hand). It will be noticed how running side increases the "throw off" of the half-ball stroke. No. 2 diagram shows how check (here also right-hand) side decreases the half-ball throw-off, the solid line representing the check side stroke. In No. 1 diagram check side would be left-hand side.

*Running side:* Increases the $\frac{1}{2}$ ball angle.

*Check side:* Decreases the $\frac{1}{2}$ ball angle.

*Pocket side:* That side which, if the cue-ball strikes the pocket jaw in a losing hazard, carries it into the pocket.

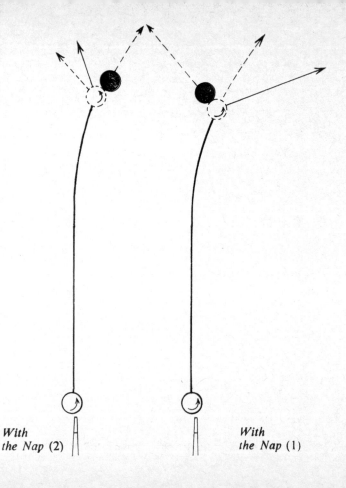

With
the Nap (2)

With
the Nap (1)

## STROKES COMBINING SIDE WITH TOP OR BOTTOM

While plain striking suffices for a large number of strokes, side and its attributes (i.e., top, bottom, stab, stun, drag, etc.) are essential for very many others, and they are often employed in combinations. Perhaps the most common example of two such elements being employed together are drag and side, and screw and side; but such matters belong to the advanced side of the games.

*Drag:* Hitting the cue-ball low, as well as with the requisite side, to make it slither and travel a distance before the side operates. If the object-ball is near the top end, drag is used to ensure true running; and as drag retards the pace of the cue-ball, the strength is not excessive. Remember that the aim is to ensure the after-position of the balls, and excessive force scatters them.

Drag is also employed with side in the two, often recurring, strokes, the Short and the Long Jenny.

The diagram illustrates both the Short and the Long Jenny, where the drag, combined with "pocket" side (in this case, left or "check"), helps to maintain the side, which causes the cue-ball to curl inwards towards the pocket opening.

*Massé stroke:* A stroke imparting a species of side by striking with uplifted cue the top area of the cue-ball, causing it to travel in a curve.

*Swerve:* Hitting the cue-ball with the cue tilted at an angle, causing it to swerve. Often used at billiards, and snooker, when it is desired to cause the cue-ball to swerve round a ball intervening between it (the cue-ball) and the ball the player intends to contact.

## MISCELLANEOUS SHOTS

*Full ball contact:* Causing the cue-ball to contact the object-ball dead in the middle.

*A fine stroke or "cut":* A glancing stroke just contacting the "outside edge" of the object-ball.

*Kiss Cannon:* The most common form is a cushion kiss cannon (as in diagram). "In the open," however, the cue-ball contacts the first object-ball, causing it to "kiss" the second, which, in its turn, is overtaken and contacted by the cue-ball.

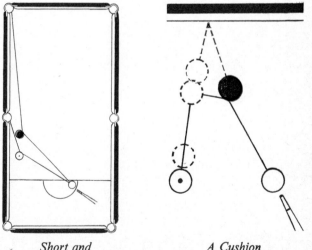

*Short and Long Jenny*

*A Cushion Kiss Cannon*

# SNOOKER

## THE GAME

Snooker is a game of skill, which originated from Pyramids and Pool, both of which it has superseded. So far as technique is concerned, every shot in snooker is part of billiards technique.

Whereas billiards offers three ways of scoring, snooker has only one: the winning hazard. In short, it is a "potting" game. The other important and characteristic element is "snookering," which is a means of obstructing your opponent.

Few good billiard players care for four-handed (i.e., two against two) billiards, but four-handed snooker is immensely popular as snooker is a game of less continuity and each player's turn to play is much more frequent.

The baulk area is a "safety" zone in billiards, but it lacks this function in snooker; and the baulk-line itself, apart from that portion which forms part of the "D," appears in the game only because it belongs to billiards. The "D" serves the same purpose as it does in billiards: that is, the player plays from it when he is "in hand" and he is always in hand after his opponent's ball has entered a pocket (which is a foul). Also, at the start of the game, the first player plays from the "D." In snooker, the ball may be played in any direction from the "D."

Twenty-two balls are used. These are the cue-ball, which each player uses in turn, 15 red balls and 6 pool or coloured balls (called the "colours"), which are yellow, green, brown, blue, pink and black.

The object of the game is to pot all the balls in succession as follows: first, pot a red ball, then a colour (any the player fancies), then a red again, then again a colour, and so on until all the 15 reds are pocketed. The reds remain in the pocket each time they are potted, but a coloured ball is retrieved from the pocket and replaced on its respective spot each time. Consequently, after all the red balls have been cleared from the table, the 6 colours remain. These must be potted in the following order: yellow, green, brown, blue, pink, black. This time each colour remains in the pocket when potted. After the black is disposed of, the game is finished, the winner being he who has gained the higher number of points. Points are scored as follows: for potting a red ball – 1 point; for potting yellow – 2; green – 3; brown – 4; blue – 5; pink – 6; black – 7.

Such a game is actually called a "frame" (of snooker), and a match consists of a given number of frames, which may be anything from the "best of three frames" up to the best of 141, lasting two weeks, as used to be the custom in some big professional contests.

The balls are placed or set up in the manner of the diagram. As can be seen in the diagram, the 15 red balls form a pyramid or triangular pack (hence the expression

"to break the pack," i.e., to disturb the opening forma-
tion of red balls). The six colours go on their respective
spots as shown, and while reds are still left on the table,
are replaced in such spots each time after they have been
potted, as previously explained. A triangular wooden
frame, the "triangle," enables the reds to be set up as
shown. The top red should be as near as possible to the
Pink without touching it.

## EXAMPLES OF A BREAK IN SNOOKER

Player pots a red (1), total 1 – then blue (5), total 6 –
another red (1), total 7 – then pink (6), total 13 – another
red (1), total 14 – green (3), total 17 – a red again (1), total
18 – the black (7), total 25, whereupon he misses a red
pot. Break 25, and his opponent takes his turn, playing
from the position left, and being on a red.

*Note.* To be "on" a ball means it is the ball the player
must "lawfully" play at: e.g., while reds are on the table,
each time a player takes his turn he is "on" a red;
having potted it, he is "on" a colour. Each time a
player fails to score (i.e., pot the ball "on") his opponent
takes his place at the table.

The highest possible break at snooker is 147, but if
the first player fouls and snookers his opponent on the
reds in his opening shot, the latter, taking a colour as
a "free" ball, then potting the black, can score 8 points
prior to starting on the reds, thus scoring 155 – but it
has never been done! 147 is scored thus: 15 reds – 15
points, 15 blacks – 105, plus the colours (2, 3, 4, 5, 6,
7) – 27, or, 15 plus 105 plus 27 equals 147.

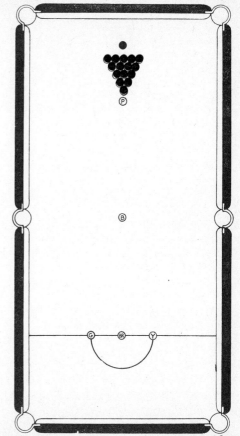

## THE OPENING SHOTS

The two favourite types of opening the game are shown here. No. 1 is still favoured by a small number of amateurs. No. 2 is the favourite professional stroke, and most good amateurs also adopt it. The advantage of No. 2 is that the cue-ball, crossing the table as it does, is more likely to remain on or near the bottom cushion (that is achieving the desired aim of making things awkward for the opponent), and it is less likely to collide with any of the three bottom colours.

No. 1 can be made without "side" (see page 22); No. 2 needs a fair amount of side (right hand) and is, therefore, more difficult. The stroke can also be made on the left, of course.

No. 1 shot makes thin contact on the end red of the 5-group, generally returning to "baulk" right of the yellow, as shown. Too thick contact may cause brown to be hit on the return. The object, as stated, is to lie on or near the bottom cushion, or, if rebounding off the cushion, behind one of the three "D" colours.

No. 2 contacts the end red of the second row (4-group). Two risks must be guarded against:
 (a)  If the red is hit too thinly, the blue may be hit on the return journey.
 (b)  If the red in front (3-group) is also hit, the cue-ball may end in the top pocket (a foul).

As no ball can be potted, except by accident, the aim of both strokes is to leave the opponent as awkwardly situated as possible when he takes his turn.

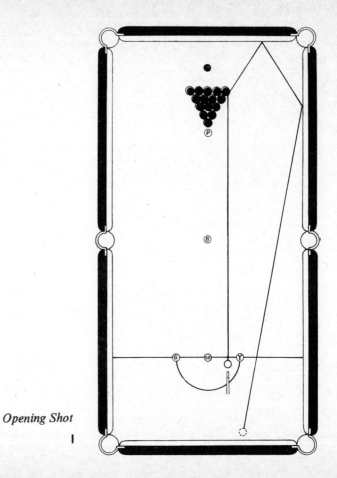

*Opening Shot*

1

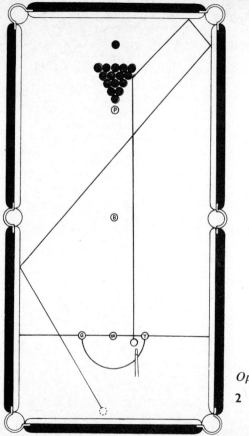

*Opening Shot*

**2**

## SNOOKERING

(Called "Laying a Snooker" or, for short, "Snooker.")

Snookering, which indeed gives the game its name, is so important that its significance must be understood at the outset. A player is "snookered" when he is prevented from hitting the ball "on" by a direct stroke because of obstruction by another ball which is not "on." Such a position is illustrated in the diagrams on page 29.

In each case, the opponent's only way to "get out of the snooker" is to play off a cushion or cushions, but, in so doing, it is probable he will hit a ball not "on" or miss altogether, thereby suffer a penalty and the player who laid the snooker will probably have a good opening. A massé stroke (see page 23) could be attempted in case 3, but this stroke is well performed by very few players.

Snookering is an integral part of the game. It is "defensive tactics," but, as it invariably leads to an opening, it can legitimately be called offensive, as to "tie up" your opponent by one, two or more such strokes gives you the initiative, his efforts to escape from (or, to "get out of") the snookers by roundabout (indirect) strokes (i.e., contacting cushions – as he is unable to hit the ball "on" directly because of interposing balls, i.e., "snookers", landing him in difficulties.

Snookering is not the whole of defensive or tactical play, since if you cannot snooker, you can play another stroke which makes things awkward for your opponent. This consists of sending the cue-ball to a spot far distant from the ball "on" (that is, the one your opponent must play at), which generally means the other end of the table. Supposing several reds are left, and there is no scoring

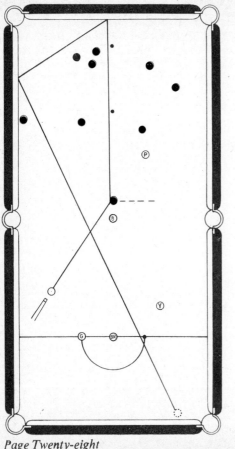

*Snooker*

**Return to bottom end of Table**

stroke discernible, it is policy to direct the cue-ball to a part of the table remote from the reds and, if possible, behind a colour (i.e., a snooker); but if no snooker is possible or, if possible, is not achieved, the mere fact of having placed the cue-ball far away from the ball "on" handicaps the opponent. This type of stroke (i.e., to the far or opposite end of the table to the ball "on") is a constant feature of the game.

After the shot shown in the diagram, the opponent must strike the cue-ball when it is close up against the cushion, which makes accuracy of cueing and direction difficult. His only course, in this position, is to execute a "safety" shot himself; but no red is nicely contactable, and the player will, therefore, probably come to grief over the stroke, and leave his ball amongst the reds, that is, in favourable position for his opponent to pot several balls. This "return to baulk" stroke is productive of many a good opening, and is especially favoured in the early stages of the game, when the table is crowded. As will be seen, there was no red favourably placed for potting. Therefore, the player executes the "return to baulk" or bottom cushion stroke.

*Snooker* 1. This diagram shows a snooker after the opening shot, the player having disturbed the pack and rebounded off the bottom cushion to lie behind the brown, thus preventing his opponent from hitting a red ball except off a cushion or cushions – a shot that may easily land him in trouble.

*Snooker* 2. Shows a snooker at an advanced stage of the game (the other balls, playing no part in the snooker, are not shown). Player is "snookered" on red by green.

*Snooker* 3. Placing red other side of blue, and cue-ball on the near side of it, thus snookering opponent on the red (by the blue), supposing this red to be the last one left on the table, the others having been potted

# THREE EXAMPLES OF "SNOOKERING"

*Snooker 1*

*Snooker 2*

*Snooker 3*

# THE "SHOT TO NOTHING"

In the early and middle stages of a "frame," an important advantage can be gained by what is called a "shot to nothing." If the player succeeds in potting a red when executing the "return to baulk," he is then on a colour and has the advantage of snookering behind a colour lying in the baulk area, by creeping slowly up to it (though he must hit it, otherwise the stroke is a miss and forfeits points). The diagrams show an example of this.

In the first, the player pots red and returns to baulk area. In the second, where an attempt to pot yellow from such a distance might be risky, he prefers to snooker behind green. His opponent, therefore, is snookered on the reds. This advantage follows from the previous stroke, i.e., "the shot to nothing," by which a red has been potted.

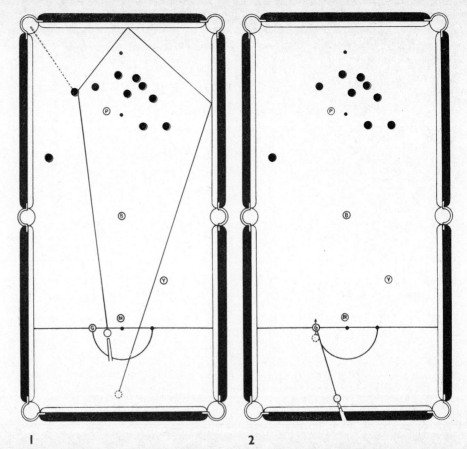

1          2

# NOMINATING A BALL

To nominate is to state aloud which ball the player is "on" (i.e., intends to hit). Ordinarily, he need only do this when some doubt exists. For instance, when, having potted a red, he aims in the direction of two colours very close to each other, if he does not nominate, the referee cannot tell which colour he meant to hit. But where no doubt exists, he need not nominate.

After a foul by his opponent, which leaves him snookered on the ball "on", a player need only nominate which ball he intends to play when requested to do so by the referee. This amendment to the original rule which stated that a player must nominate after being awarded a "free" ball came into operation as from 1st December, 1973. He is still advised to do so for his own protection. Should a player not nominate after being awarded a "free" ball, the ball he plays is deemed to be the nominated ball, but should he nominate a ball he must hit that ball otherwise it would be a foul. Thus, if he is on a red, and is unable to hit it directly, he may choose ("nominate") a colour, as a red. This is generally referred to as a "free ball" (though the expression does not figure in the official rules). The player must hit the nominated ball or it is a foul. The nominated or "free" ball acquires the numerical value of the ball "on." Thus, nominating black for a red, the black counts as 1 point only, if potted. In the same way, after the reds are disposed of, the player may nominate any other colour when he is snookered by a foul. The "free" ball must be re-spotted, if potted, in any case.

Years ago, the player was allowed to use the nominated ball to snooker his opponent in turn, but the modern rule forbids this, and if he uses the "free" or nominated ball to snooker, it is a foul, except when only pink and black remain on the table.

If he pots the nominated (or "free") ball he scores the value of the ball "on," as stated. If he fails to pot the nominated ball but pots the ball "on" he scores its value, e.g., nominating green as red, he fails to pot green, but pots red. He scores one point and continues his break. If he pots both he scores the value of the ball "on" only, and continues. Again, if he pots both, the nominated ball *only* must be re-spotted. In any case he *must* hit the nominated ball.

*Note.* Two reds, when a red is the ball "on" can be potted in the same stroke. Two reds may be hit simultaneously, so may the nominated ball and the ball "on," but in no other case may two balls be hit simultaneously.

# BALLS TOUCHING

If the cue-ball is touching a ball not "on", the player must play away from it, without moving it. He must hit the ball "on" and must not hit another ball.

If the cue-ball is touching a ball which is "on," he must also play away from it without moving it. He need not hit another ball, nor is it a foul if he strikes another ball.

He may even pocket a ball which is "on" but not one which is not "on."

## GENERAL STRATEGY OF SNOOKER

The chief aim is to pot the balls, of course, and there are players who concentrate on "potting" and do not worry about leaving the balls "on" for their opponent (i.e., favourably placed) if they miss. Potters of exceptional ability, therefore, go all out to pot the balls as quickly as possible, but they often come to grief against a calculating player who sets out to make things difficult for them by leaving the cue-ball in awkward positions, and by laying snookers whenever possible. Two or three skilful defensive shots, including a snooker or two, will often bring a player a winning opening. Some players are supremely gifted in potting, and when their eye is in, they can win a frame in no time; but the greatest players are those who, like the foremost professionals and amateurs, combine good potting with calculated craft and tactics, and await their opportunities.

Positional play is all-important in snooker, and it lies in the ability to pot a ball and get into perfect position to pot the next ball. In so doing, the player may have to pot a red at the bottom end and get to the other end for position on a colour. This he must do in such a way that he does not collide with other balls. A knowledge of the "angles" (i.e., contacts with the cushions) is therefore indispensable.

## FOULS

He must not :-

(*a*) **Direct** the cue-ball into a pocket ("go **in-off**"), **whether** it strikes another ball, or balls, or not.

(*b*) Miss altogether (i.e., not contact a ball with the cue-ball). Unscrupulous players sometimes make a "miss" intentionally to avoid getting in a bad position, or to get back to a safe position. A repetition of this offence may lead to disqualification; the referee may also order the stroke to be replayed.

(*c*) Pot a ball out of the correct order (i.e., one which is not "on"), such as potting one red, then another red, instead of a colour.

(*d*) Play with a ball other than a cue-ball.

(*e*) Touch a ball with a part of the cue other than the tip or with some part of his dress, hand, etc.

(*f*) Force a ball, or balls, off the table.

(*g*) Fail to hit the ball nominated by him after the opponent's foul.

(*h*) Move a ball which is touching the cue-ball, instead of playing away from it without moving it.

(*i*) Strike two balls simultaneously other than two red balls, or the nominated ball and the ball "on."

(*j*) Snooker with the nominated ball, except when only pink and black remain.

(*k*) Push with the cue-tip instead of striking.

(*l*) Play before the balls have come to rest.

## PENALTIES

The penalties for the various fouls are given in the official Rule Book, but, as a general principle, the penalties for most fouls are calculated according to the values of the balls involved in the foul, the forfeit being the value of the highest. As the minimum penalty is 4 points, it follows that the forfeit-value of the red, yellow and green balls will be 4 in each case, not 1, 2, and 3 respectively. There is also a rule which declares that the first impact governs all strokes, but this does not always apply if two fouls are involved in the stroke.

Examples of foul awards:

Player, "on" red, strikes black .. 7 points forfeit (or, as it is commonly called, "7 away").

Player, "on" black, strikes red .. 7 points forfeit *Note*. In each case "black," value 7, is the higher value and this, therefore, determines the forfeit.

Player, "on" red, misses red and strikes blue .. 5 away (blue, 5, is higher than 4, red forfeit value).

In any foul, therefore, the process of assessing the forfeit value should be: count "first impact" value, then ball "on" value, then value of ball "wrongfully struck," "wrongfully pocketed," etc., and the highest is the forfeit value of the foul.

Here are some examples:

Player "on" blue, misses blue, strikes green, then cue-ball, still moving, contacts pink, which enters a pocket and player then fouls black with his cue. First impact was on green, ball not "on" – "4 away;" ball "on" (blue) was missed, "5 away," which cancels first impact forfeit (green 4); pink "wrongfully pocketed" means a forfeit of 6 points, which cancels the blue forfeit, and then we come to black, forfeit value 7. This cancels pink, therefore 7 is the forfeit for this example.

Player pots yellow, and after cue-ball has stopped, fouls pink with cue. Penalty: 6 points, yellow re-spotted.

Player snookers with the nominated ball. Penalty: value of ball "on"; thus, player chooses black, as nominated ball after a foul, ball "on" being green. He snookers with black. Penalty: 4 points.

Black is ball "on." Player hits black, which cannons on to blue, potting it. Penalty: 7 points, highest numerical value, blue 5, but black 7.

Player, "on" a red, hits it, but then strikes black and goes in-off (i.e., into pocket). Penalty: 4 points. First impact (which governs all strokes) was on red, for which the penalty is 4 (4 being the minimum penalty).

Player, "on" a red, is snookered after a foul. He nominates black, fails to hit it and strikes a red, also potting black. Penalty: 4 points, as black, the nominated ball, acquired the value of red, for which it was nominated. Therefore, it takes the penalty value of red, viz., 4.

*Snooker*

# DEFINITIONS

HALF-BALL ANGLE. In snooker, this has importance, just as in billiards, but only insofar as it concerns the course of the object-ball (as potting, and not a losing hazard, is concerned). In billiards the object-ball takes an angle of 30 degrees in the half-ball loser. When, therefore, the player detects a ball at an angle of 30 degrees from a pocket, he can pot it by striking it half-ball.

"IT'S (ALL) ON THE BLACK." This means that the scores of the two players are 7 or less points apart. Therefore, whoever pots the black will (if 7 points behind) draw level; if 6 or less behind, win the game. An "on the black" game ends also if one player fouls (and thus forfeits 7), the rule stating: "The first score or forfeit ends the game." If the potting of the black brings the scores level, the black is spotted, and the players toss for choice whether to play, or to ask the opponent to play.

"WANTING A SNOOKER." This means a player cannot win except by making his opponent forfeit points. For example, "A" leads "B" by 50 to 30 points, and only blue, pink and black remain (18 points). If "B" pots all three balls, his score will be 48, so that he will still be the loser. If, however, he can lay a snooker and cause his opponent to miss, go in-off, etc., he will have the benefit of the points forfeited by his opponent. Suppose it is a snooker on the blue – the ball "on" in the prescribed sequence of potting the colours: he will be awarded 5 points; thus, with the 3 balls (18 points plus 5) he will be able to win 53-50, provided, of course, "A" does not score again. He thus "wants one snooker" (in such a position of the scores).

"TAKING THE COLOURS." When all the reds have been potted, the colours, of course, remain, and sometimes they will be nearly all (or even all) still on their spots. To "take the colours" means, therefore, to pot them in one break in numerical rotation, i.e., from yellow to black, whether some or all are on their spots or not.

SET or PLANT. The two terms have become practically synonymous. Generally speaking, they apply to a position in which two reds are touching one another. In such a position it is possible to pot one or other of the balls by contacting, in the one case, the ball nearer the pocket, or, in the other, the further one. In the first instance, a squeeze between the cue-ball and the second object-ball achieves the pot; in the other, correct contact on the ball further from the pocket gives the necessary direction to the one nearer the pocket.

## TWO NEW RULES

The "Jump Shot," by which the cue-ball is made to leap over any ball by hitting it very low down, is now a foul. **(Both games.)**

SNOOKER: After a foul stroke by his opponent, a player may play from the position left (with a free ball, if snookered) or ask his opponent to play the next stroke. If the latter, when playing again, fouls a second time, he may be asked to play again a second time, but if he does not foul again, he may not be so requested.

*Page Thirty-four*

# VOLUNTEER SNOOKER

Volunteer Snooker is a variation of the normal snooker game which is easy to play and appeals to those who have no wish to master the real game.

The balls are set out exactly as in snooker but whereas in snooker the player's task is to pot a red and then a colour, and when reds are all potted, the colours in rotation, in Volunteer Snooker, after potting a red and then a colour the player may take another colour out of its proper order; this colour must be named and is then said to have been "volunteered" by the player. For example, suppose you have potted a red and pink, you may now declare or volunteer any other colour you wish by naming it. This ball would, of course, be the easiest one to pot after the pink. If you fail to pot your volunteered ball you forfeit its value (7 if black, 6 if pink, 5 blue, etc.) to your opponent. This risk naturally imparts an extra element of expectancy to the game. If, however, you pot the volunteered ball three times in succession in the same turn it remains off the table until the next stroke. For this next stroke a red or any colour may be chosen and it is "free." That is there is no penalty if you fail to pot it.

You may not "volunteer" a ball until you have lawfully potted a red in each visit or turn at the table. If a player who lawfully pockets the last red ball pockets any pool ball by his next stroke, the latter ball is respotted. A red ball is always free, that is you may play on it. If the reds are all off the table then the next ball to be played is the ball which is on.

It is obvious from the above that reckless play can be expensive and to volunteer a ball which is difficult to pot is obviously unwise. It is better to take the easier chances.

As in snooker, the player must have ability to pot with confidence.

Apart from the "volunteering" element, the game is subject to the same rules as snooker and the player must know the rules of both games to play properly.

# RUSSIAN POOL

This game is also called Indian Pool, Toad-in-the-Hole or Slosh and is another of the many subsidiary games which add to the enjoyment of the billiard table. It is a combination of billiards and snooker and its "free-scoring" possibilities make it a pleasant diversion, especially for players who are not very skilled at either billiards or snooker.

There are five balls in the game: white (the cue ball), yellow, green, blue and black. Black goes on the billiard spot (that is the one on which the red ball is placed at the beginning of billiards), blue on the centre spot; green on the left hand and the yellow on the right hand corner of the D. The ball values are as follows: black, when potted or the object of a losing hazard, 9 points; blue 7; green 5; yellow 3. The scoring of the game is by winning or losing hazards, that is pots or in-offs, scoring as explained and also by cannons which score two points. Consecutive direct cannons on the same two balls are limited to 25 and after this the player must make a hazard or a direct cannon, that is one from ball to ball. He may also continue his break after 25 cannons if he makes a direct cannon in conjunction with a hazard or a cannon in which at least one of the balls is different from those of the 25 cannons referred to. With the high ball values for hazards, scoring can be quite high compared with billiards or snooker. For example, by cannoning from black to blue, combined with pocketing black in top pocket and blue in centre pocket, you can score 18 points in one stroke. You may not, however, pot the balls in *any* pocket; black can be potted only into the two top pockets; blue only into the two centre pockets and green and yellow into the two bottom pockets. This rule also applies to losing hazards (in-offs). Not more than three consecutive winning hazards of the same ball off the same spot may be made without conjunction of another score. The game is started with the black ball being struck by direct contact.

The cannon, although its value is only 2, is a valuable stroke for scoring as many opportunities for cannon sequence occur so that skill at cannon play is a valuable asset in the game. A sequence in scoring is helped by ability to manoeuvre the balls when making a cannon sequence, towards a pocket permitting a losing or winning hazard. The game gives scope for positional play and it is advantageous to concentrate on controlling your first ball when making a cannon, and the possibility of manoeuvring from cannons to hazards is a fascinating aspect of the game. As the scores are high so are the penalties and it is obviously not much use scoring abundantly if you make many mistakes.

Russian Pool is sometimes played with an extra ball, pink, which is spotted on the pyramid spot and is called the "Rover." With pink, winning or losing hazards may be made in any pocket and score 6 points. Pink may, of course, be used for cannon play (2 points). The aim of the game, as with billiards and snooker, is to score more points up to a figure mutually agreed upon by the players.

The rules of Volunteer Snooker and Russian Pool are included with those of Billiards and Snooker in the official handbook and rules published by the Billiards Association and Control Council. These are worth buying.

## BILLIARDS GOLF

The Billiards Association and Control Council do not issue rules for this game but they may be briefly stated as follows:

The red ball is placed on the centre spot or the billiards spot as agreed upon by the players.

All players start in hand from the "D."

The object of the game is to pot the red ball into all the pockets commencing with the left hand top pocket continuing with the right hand top pocket, the right hand middle pocket, the right hand bottom pocket, the left hand bottom pocket, to finish at the sixth hole that is the left hand middle pocket. The red when potted is placed on the spot agreed upon and the player's cue ball must be played from where it has come to rest, whether the red has been potted or not.

The player who takes the lowest number of strokes to accomplish the task wins the game. The penalties are a missed turn if you make a miss, or a losing hazard, even if it is in conjunction with a winning hazard.

Fifteen is a good performance and 6, of course, the best possible.

The game is excellent practice to improve your positional play sense, for when the red is potted into the correct stipulated pocket the player must try to leave the cue ball as favourably placed as he can to pot the red into the next pocket and so on. This requires a good standard of cue ball control.

   Printed in Great Britain by Sunstreet Printing Works (Keighley) Ltd., Keighley, Yorks.